Crocheted
PURSENALITIES

CROCHETED
Pursenalities

20 GREAT FELTED BAGS

Eva Wiechmann

Martingale®
& COMPANY

Crocheted Pursenalities: 20 Great Felted Bags
© 2007 by Eva Wiechmann

Martingale & Company®
20205 144th Ave. NE
Woodinville, WA 98072-8478
www.martingale-pub.com

Printed in China
12 11 10 09 08 07   8 7 6 5 4 3 2 1

Library of Congress Cataloging-in-Publication Data
Library of Congress Control Number: 2007001177

ISBN: 978-1-56477-750-8

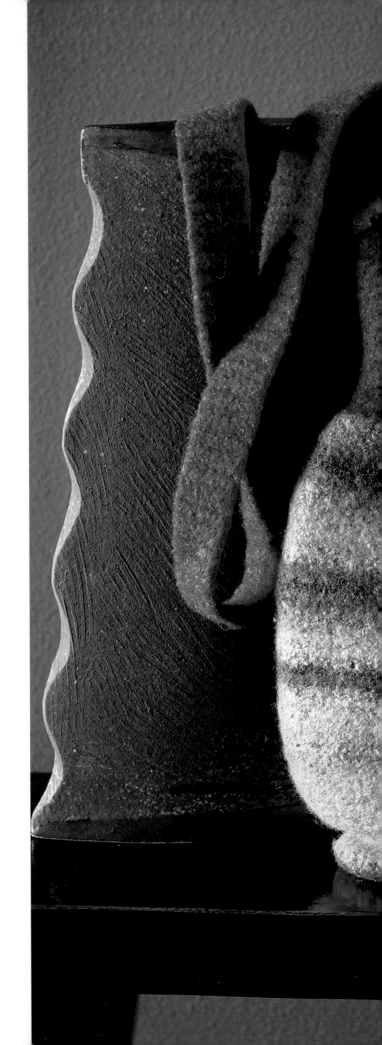

CREDITS

CEO   Tom Wierzbicki

Publisher   Jane Hamada

Editorial Director   Mary V. Green

Managing Editor   Tina Cook

Technical Editor   Ursula Reikes

Copy Editor   Liz McGehee

Design Director   Stan Green

Illustrator   Laurel Strand

Cover and Text Designer   Shelly Garrison

Photographer   Brent Kane

MISSION STATEMENT

Dedicated to providing quality products and service to inspire creativity.

DEDICATION

To your dreams—because without a dream,
you can't have your dreams come true.

ACKNOWLEDGMENTS

As always, my heartfelt thanks to all the people who had to put up with me during this production and who did not lose their calm (I realize it was not always easy).

Thanks to Martingale & Company for giving me yet another task (I mean chance). *Crocheted Pursenalities* was a challenge, but well worth it. Also, my heartfelt thanks to Ursula Reikes, who always keeps me on track.

Thanks once again to my friends, customers, and helpers, who did not get tired of bringing in new ideas when my brain was fried and nothing was coming out of it.

Contents

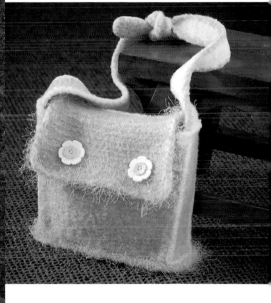

Introduction

When I was asked to design a collection of crocheted bags, I realized that I had ignored (not intentionally) a huge audience. Not only is felting hot, but crocheting is experiencing a comeback (was it ever gone?) just as knitting has over the past few years. My sincere apologies to the crocheting world, experts and beginners alike. My only concern was that I might not be able to make the bags just as tailored and fashionable as the knitted ones, but I have found it is possible to make crocheted felting look great! As I created each one, I got more excited about the possibilities. Hopefully, you will like the results. Please consider these patterns as guidelines—pick up an idea and add your own personal touch to them. Be creative and have fun. The sky is the limit. Crochet on!

After the last bag was felted, cleaned up, and embellished and the leftover yarns, buttons, grommets, and tools were put away—there was a table and a floor under all that stuff—the house felt almost empty. There were 20 bags lined up, but something was missing. My babies didn't have names. So I hung them up in the store and let my customers decide what name to give each of them. I got some wonderful ideas. Thanks to everyone who participated!

—Eva

Getting Started

Felting is a wonderfully amazing process. You can create something that's beautiful, practical, and durable at the same time.

It's like cooking: you need 100% wool that is not a superwash as your main ingredient, some basic working tools, and all sorts of add-ons and novelties for spice.

The bags are crocheted loosely with a lot larger hook than you would normally use for the yarn. These are great beginning projects since your stitches don't have to be perfect. Felting "melts" everything together and does not show the imperfections.

Once the bags are completed, the felting can begin. A washing machine is an important part of the production of these bags. If you have a front-loading machine, refer to the manufacturer's instructions for information on how to stop the wash cycle before it goes into the rinse and spin cycles. Here are some basic guidelines you should follow to make the bag wonderful.

1. Place your bag in a mesh garment bag or pillowcase before putting it in the washing machine. Don't crowd or fold the bag if it's too large to fit in either of the above. Put it in the machine without it.

2. Add a little no-rinse wool wash (such as Eucalan) to speed the process.

3. Add hot water and turn on the machine; it's the agitation that does the trick, not the hot water alone.

4. Do *not* let the machine go into a spin cycle. It can create permanent creases!

5. Check on the bag regularly. This is very important! Straighten out the corners, bottoms, flaps, and handles. Pull and tug to keep the shape it should be. Different yarns and colors felt differently, so don't assume that one bag is like the other.

6. Put the bag back in and repeat the cycle from the beginning as many times as it takes to achieve satisfying results.

7. Squeeze out the water. Roll the bag between towels to get the moisture out.

8. Shape the bag again. Make sure everything is lined up and even. Stuff with newspaper or plastic bags to keep the shape, and hang it up to dry.

9. As it is drying, keep checking on the bag to make sure everything is even. Reshape as needed.

10. Last but not least, shave the bag a lot. Shaving gets rid of the extra fuzz, and colors become nice and clear. Use disposable razors. Please do not borrow your husband's; it will get you in trouble.

Taking care of your felted bags is simple. Shave away any fuzz and pilling that might occur from use. If necessary, wash the bag in cold water, reshape, stuff with paper, and hang to dry. You can also felt your bag again if it gets stretched out of shape.

Top: Before felting.
Bottom: The shaved portion is on the right, and the unshaved portion is on the left.

Crochet Basics

A few crochet basics are provided to help you get started.

GAUGE

Gauge is not too important. With one strand of yarn and an M hook, you should get approximately nine single crochet stitches in 4". With two strands of yarn held together and a P hook, you should get approximately seven single crochet stitches in 4".

STITCHES

Simple stitches are used for these bags, which makes them perfect for beginners.

Slip Stitch (sl st): A slip stitch is used to move across one or more stitches that won't be used again. Insert the hook into the stitch, yarn over the hook, and pull through both stitches at once.

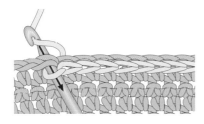

Single Crochet (sc): Insert the hook into the chain or stitch indicated, yarn over the hook, and pull through the chain or stitch (two loops remain on hook).

Yarn over the hook and pull through the remaining two loops on the hook.

Single Crochet Increase: Work two single crochet stitches into the same stitch.

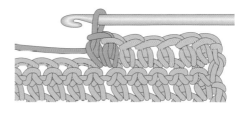

Single Crochet Decrease: (Insert hook into the next stitch, yarn over, pull up a loop) twice; yarn over and pull through all three loops on the hook.

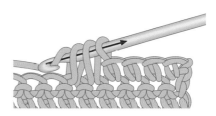

Double Crochet (dc): Yarn over the hook, insert hook into chain or stitch indicated. *Yarn over the hook and pull through the stitch (three loops are on hook); yarn over the hook and pull through two loops on hook (two loops remain on hook).

Yarn over the hook and pull through the remaining two loops on hook (one loop remains on hook).

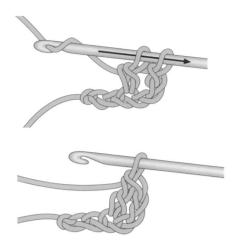

Reverse Single Crochet: This stitch is worked from left to right instead of from right to left. When you get to the end of the row, chain 1, do not turn; *insert hook into stitch at right, yarn over the hook, draw through a loop, yarn over the hook, and draw through 2 loops on hook. Repeat from * across the row. Fasten off.

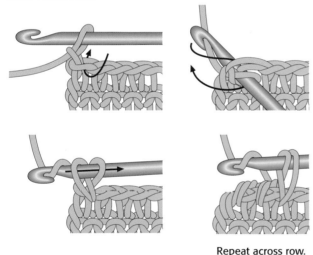

Repeat across row.

WORKING IN LOOPS

Stitches can be worked in the front loops, back loops, or both loops of the stitches from the previous row. Pay attention to the directions to make sure you are working in the correct portion of the stitch.

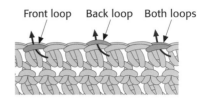

Front loop   Back loop   Both loops

CHANGING YARN COLOR

To change colors, work the last stitch of the old color until two loops remain on the hook. Drop the old yarn. Pick up the new yarn and pull it through the last two loops on the hook. Cut the old yarn and crochet in the tails with the next few stitches.

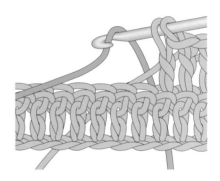

WORKING IN THE ROUND

Most bags are worked in a spiral. This means that they are worked in the round but that there is no chain at the beginning of a round and no slip stitch to join at the end of a round unless otherwise indicated. Mark the beginning of a round by placing a split-ring marker in the first stitch. Remove and replace the marker in each subsequent round. If a pattern requires more than one marker, use a different-colored marker to indicate the beginning of the round.

WORKING BACK AND FORTH

Flaps, handles, and straps are worked back and forth. The chain 1 at the beginning of a row of single crochet does not count as a stitch. The chain 2 at the beginning of a row of double crochet does count as a stitch.

WHIPSTITCHING SEAMS

With edges aligned and right sides together, use a tapestry needle and one strand of matching wool to whipstitch the seams, working under one loop on each piece.

WHIPSTITCHING DECORATIVE EDGES

This decorative stitch is worked with contrasting yarn. Using a tapestry needle and the designated yarn, whipstitch around the edges as indicated in the pattern. Make stitches ¼" to ½" from the edge and about ¼" to ½" apart.

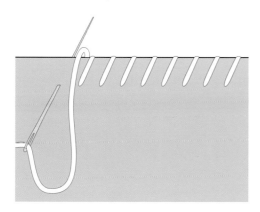

DECORATIVE CHAIN STITCH

Embroider a chain stitch on any bag to add a decorative touch.

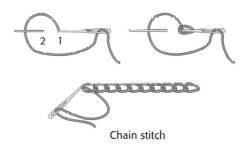

Chain stitch

POCKETS AND POCKET LININGS

Sew pockets and pocket linings to the bags after felting. Using an embroidery needle and pearl cotton or embroidery floss, whipstitch the items in place.

ZIPPERS

Sew zippers in place after felting. Use a sharp needle and matching thread for sewing. Pin the zipper in place, backstitch next to the teeth, and whipstitch along the tape edge.

SNAPS, GROMMETS, AND EYELETS

You will need to purchase a tool to attach these items. Follow the manufacturer's instructions since they vary from product to product.

DREAM of Genie

Something magical might happen if you rub the belly of this bag—
imagine ocean breezes or Italian pottery or . . .

Skill Level: Beginner ■☐☐☐

Finished Measurements after Felting
Approx 12" at widest point x 11" high x 3½" deep

MATERIALS

MC 4 balls of Karaoke from South West Trading Company (50% silk, 50% wool; 50 g; 109 m) in color 302 (4)

CC 1 skein of Cascade 220 from Cascade Yarns (100% wool; 100 g; 220 yds) in color 9457 Blue (4)

K-10½ (6.5 mm) crochet hook

M-13 (9 mm) crochet hook

Stitch marker

BAG

Beg bag at top. Use 1 strand of yarn unless otherwise instructed. Work in bls only unless otherwise instructed.

- With M hook and CC, ch 64, sl st in beg ch to join in rnd, pm to mark beg of rnd.
- Sc 6 rnds.
- Working in both loops with K hook, sc 2 rnds. Cut CC. Change to M hook and MC.
- **Inc rnd:** Working in bls, work 2 sc in each sc around—128 sts.
- Sc around until piece measures 11" from beg of MC.
- **Dec rnd:** Sc2tog around—64 sts. Cut MC.

BOTTOM

- With K hook and 2 strands of CC held tog, working in bls, sc 2 rnds.
- **Dec rnd:** (Sc2tog, sc in each of next 30 sc) twice. Fasten off. Leave tail for sewing bottom seam.

HANDLE

Work in both loops for entire handle.

- With K hook and 1 strand of CC, ch 11. Sc in second ch from hook and in each ch across—10 sts. Turn.
- Ch 1, sc in first sc and in each sc across. Turn.
- Rep last row until piece measures 2" from beg.
- **Dec row:** Ch 1, sc2tog, sc in each sc to last 2 sc, sc2tog—8 sts. Turn.
- Work even until piece measures 4" from beg.
- **Dec row:** Ch 1, sc2tog, sc in each sc to last 2 sc, sc2tog—6 sts. Turn.
- Work even until piece measures 26" from beg.
- **Inc row:** Ch 1, work 2 sc in first sc, sc in each sc to last sc, work 2 sc in last sc—8 sts. Turn.
- Work even until piece measures 28" from beg.
- **Inc row:** Ch 1, work 2 sc in first sc, sc in each sc to last sc, work 2 sc in last sc—10 sts. Turn.
- Work even until piece measures 30" from beg. Fasten off.

FINISHING

- Whipstitch ends of handle to each side of bag on top edge.
- Felt bag according to instructions on page 12.

The Karaoke color 302 felts quickly. Keep an eye on it.

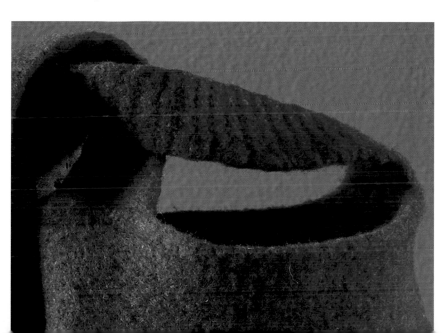

Tequila SUNRISE

Hot desert sun and a cool drink—life is good. What more can you ask for, except to find the most perfect button to go with your bag?

Skill Level: Intermediate ◼◼◼◻

Finished Measurements after Felting
Approx 14" at widest point x 10½" high x 3½" deep

MATERIALS

MC 5 skeins of Karaoke from South West Trading Company (50% soy silk, 50% wool; 50 g; 109 yds) in color 297 **(4)**

CC 1 skein of Cascade 220 from Cascade Yarns (100% wool; 100 g; 220 yds) in Heather color 2436 Orange **(4)**

K-10½ (6.5 mm) crochet hook

M-13 (9 mm) crochet hook

Stitch markers

1 antique gold buckle set

1 wooden button, 1¾" diameter

3 small eyelets in various colors

BAG

Beg bag at top. Work in bls only unless otherwise instructed.

- With M hook and 2 strands of CC, ch 70, sl st to beg ch to join into rnd, pm to mark beg of rnd. Cut 1 strand of CC; with rem strand of CC, sc 6 rnds.

- Working in both loops with K hook and 1 strand of CC, sc 2 rnds. Cut CC. Change to M hook and 1 strand of MC.

- **Inc rnd:** Working in bls, work 2 sc in first sc and in each sc around—140 sts.

- Sc around until piece measures 13" from beg of MC.

- **Dec rnd:** (Sc2tog, sc3tog) around—56 sts. Cut MC. Change to CC.

BOTTOM

- With 2 strands of CC, working in bls, sc 2 rnds; place second marker at st 29.

- **Dec rnd:** Sc2tog, sc to 2 sts from second marker, sc2tog before and after marker, sc to 2 sts from first marker, sc2tog— 52 sts.

- **Dec rnd:** Sc2tog, sc in each of next 20 sts, sc2tog 3 times, sc in each of next 20 sts, sc2tog twice—46 sts.

- Sc 1 rnd. Fasten off. Use tail to sew bottom seam.

- With 1 strand of CC, sc 1 rnd in free loops around bottom edge.

FLAP

Work in both loops throughout flap.

- With WS facing you, M hook, and 1 strand of CC, join yarn to sixth st of beg ch, sc in each of next 25 sts. Turn.

- Ch 1, sc in first st and in each st across. Turn.

- Rep last row 11 more times.

- **Dec and buttonhole row:** Ch 1, sc2tog, sc in each of next 8 sc, ch 5, sk 5 sc, sc in each of next 8 sts, sc2tog—23 sts. Turn.

- **Dec row:** Ch 1, sc2tog, sc in each sc and in each ch to last 2 sc, sc2tog—21 sts. Turn.

- Work dec row 2 more times—17 sts. Fasten off.

- With RS facing you, M hook, and 1 strand of MC, sc around flap.

HANDLE (MAKE 2)

Work in both loops throughout handle.

- With M hook and 1 strand of CC, ch 7. Sc in second ch from hook and in each ch across—6 sts. Turn.

- Ch 1, sc in first st and in each sc across. Turn.

- Rep last row to 8" for short piece, and 18" for long piece.

- Whipstitch short piece to left end at top, and long piece to right end at top.

FINISHING

- Felt bag according to instructions on page 12.

- Attach buckle and eyelets to handles.

- Sew on button.

TEXAS Hold 'em

Silver studs and trims make this little bag look very dynamic in denim.
It can hold more than you think.

Skill Level: Easy ◖■□▷

Finished Measurements after Felting
Approx 10" at widest point x 8" high x 3" deep

MATERIALS

Cascade 220 from Cascade Yarns (100% wool;
100 g; 220 yds) (**4**)

MC 1 skein in color 9325 Light Denim

CC1 1 skein in color 9326 Medium Denim

CC2 1 skein in color 8393 Navy

M-13 (9 mm) crochet hook

Stitch markers

4 horseshoe purse hooks

8 spacer beads* (large enough to fit onto purse
hooks)

8 medium grommets

16 double-cap rivets

1 oval button, 1¼" wide

*These beads are used on the wrong side of the
purse hooks to keep the corners open on the bag.

BAG

Beg bag at bottom. Use 1 strand of yarn throughout.
Work in bls only unless otherwise instructed.

- With M hook and CC1, ch 21. Sc in second ch
  from hook and in each ch to last ch, work 3 sc in
  last ch. Working on opposite side, sc in free loops
  of beg ch to last ch, work 2 sc in last ch. Pm in
  last st and in 21st st—42 sts.

- (Sc to marked st, work 3 sc in marked st) twice.
  Move marker to center sc of 3 sc in each rnd.

- Rep last rnd 4 more times—62 sts.

- Sc 1 rnd. Cut CC1. Change to MC.

- **Inc rnd:** Working in both loops (sc in next sc,
  work 2 sc in next sc) around—93 sts.

- Working in bls, sc around until piece measures
  10" from beg of MC. Cut MC.

- Change to CC1, sc 4 rnds. Cut CC1.

- Change to CC2; working in both loops, sc 1 rnd.
  Fasten off.

FLAP

Work in both loops throughout flap.

- With CC1, join yarn, sc in center 25 sts of back.
  Turn.

- Ch 1, sc in first sc and in each sc across. Turn.

- Rep last row until piece measures 3".

- **Dec row:** Ch 1, sc2tog, sc in each st to last 2 sts,
  sc2tog. Turn.

- Rep last row 6 more times—11 sts. Turn

- **Dec and buttonhole row:** Ch 1, sc2tog, sc in next 2
  sc, ch 3, sk 3, sc in next 2 sc, sc2tog—9 sts. Turn.

- Ch 1, sc in first st and in each sc and ch across.
  Fasten off.

TRIM

- For top, with CC1 and RS facing you, join yarn at
  edge of flap and working in both loops, sc around
  flap.

- For bottom, with CC2, sc 1 rnd in free loops
  around bottom edge.

HANDLES (MAKE 2)

- With CC2, ch 83 loosely. Sc in second ch from
  hook and in each ch across—82 sts. Do not turn,
  but start next 2 rows from beg with RS facing you.

- Working in both loops, sc 1 row with CC1, then 1
  row with CC2. Fasten off each color at end of row.
  Weave in ends.

FINISHING

- Felt bag and handles according to instructions on
  page 12.

- Insert 2 grommets in each corner, spaced approx
  1½" apart.

- Attach purse hooks in each
  corner, placing 2 spacer
  beads on WS.

- Sew handles to purse
  hooks.

- Attach rivets and sew on
  button.

Canteen

This bag is way too pretty to take on a hike. The Strass stones embellish and dress up this little shoulder bag.

Skill Level: Intermediate ◖■■◻

Finished Measurements after Felting
Approx 5" wide at top and bottom, 10" wide at middle x 8" high x 2" deep

MATERIALS

Cascade 220 from Cascade Yarns (100% wool; 100 g; 220 yds) **4**

MC 2 skeins in Quatro color 5018 Turquoise

CC 1 skein in color 9421 Turquoise

M-13 (9 mm) crochet hook

Stitch marker

2 square ¾" white buckles

6 small white eyelets

GGH Strass stones*, 12 teardrops and 4 circles, color 002

1 nonmagnetic snap, silver

Needle and thread to match yarn

*Strass stones have holes in them and are sewn on, not ironed on.

PATTERN STITCH

Row 1 (WS): Ch 1; working in fls, sc in first st and in each sc across. Turn.

Row 2 (RS): Ch 1; working in bls, sc in first st and in each sc across. Turn.

BAG FRONT

Beg bag at center. Use 1 strand of yarn throughout. Work in bls only unless otherwise instructed.

- With MC, ch 2, work 6 sc in second ch from hook, sl st in first sc. Pm in last st worked and move marker each rnd.

- Work 2 sc in each sc around—12 sts.

- (Sc in next sc, work 2 sc in next sc) around—18 sts.

- (Sc in each of next 2 sc, work 2 sc in next sc) around—24 sts.

- (Sc in each of next 3 sc, work 2 sc in next sc) around—36 sts.

- Cont in this manner, working 1 more sc between inc, until you complete (sc in each of next 20 sc, 2 sc in next sc) around—132 sts. Front has 6 corners.

BAG BACK

Work as for front, except start with 7 sc in second chain and work 7 inc in each round—154 sts after last round. Back has 7 corners.

GUSSET

- With CC, ch 20. With RS of front piece facing you and beg at one corner, sc across 110 sts, ch 20—150 sts. Turn.

  Work patt st until gusset measures 3", ending with WS row and leaving last 20 sts unworked (these 20 sts form handle). Turn.

- **Join back piece:** With WS facing each other, sc back loops of gusset tog with front loops of back piece. Leave last 20 sts unworked, but cont sc around last point of back piece (this becomes flap). Turn at end of flap; working in both loops, sc around flap. Fasten off.

TRIM

With RS facing you, join CC to front edge of bag; working in both loops, sc across front; then working in free loops, sc around front side of gusset. Fasten off.

STRAP

- With CC, ch 61 very loosely. Sc in second ch from hook and in each ch across to last ch, work 2 sc in last ch; working along opposite side, sc in free loops of beg ch to last ch, work 2 sc in last ch.

- Sc 1 rnd. Fasten off.

FINISHING

- Felt bag and handle according to instructions on page 12.

- Attach eyelets to each end of strap, and buckles to handles.

- Sew Strass stones to front with needle and matching thread.

- Attach snap to flap and front of bag.

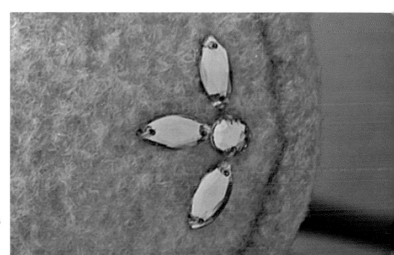

Autumn LEAVES

Autumn in the forest and a little fuzzy-wuzzy—to think that I almost discarded this creation. But once it got pockets, cute handles, and was cleaned up, it became my favorite.

Skill Level: Easy ◀■□▷

Finished Measurements after Felting
Approx 8½" wide x 8" high x 6" deep

MATERIALS

MC 3 skeins of 127 Print from Filatura di Crosa (100% wool; 50 g; 93 yds) in color 27 (**4**)

CC1 1 skein of Cascade 220 from Cascade Yarns (100% wool, 100 g; 220 yds) in Heather color 2435 Brown (**4**)

CC2 1 skein of Fizz Stardust from Crystal Palace Yarns (86% polyester, 14% lurex; 50 g; 120 yds) in color 4423 Ginger (**3**)

M-13 (9 mm) crochet hook

Stitch marker

1 card of Rainbow Gallery Super Suede in Brown

1 pair of round wooden handles, 5" diameter

1 wooden button, 1" diameter

Needle and embroidery floss to match CC1

PATTERN STITCH

Row 1 (WS): Ch 1; working in fls, sc in first st and in each sc across. Turn.

Row 2 (RS): Ch 1; working in bls, sc in first st and in each sc across. Turn.

BAG

Beg bag at bottom. Work in bls only unless otherwise instructed.

- With 2 strands of CC1 held tog, ch 31. Sc in second ch from hook and in each ch across—30 sts. Turn.

- Ch 1, sc in first st and in each sc across. Turn.

- Rep last row until piece measures 9" from beg. Do not turn at end of last row.

- Turn piece 90° to right; work 20 sc in ends of rows, 30 sc in free loops of beg ch, 20 sc in opposite ends of rows—100 sts. Pm to mark beg of rnd. Cut CC1.

- Change to 1 strand of MC. Sc until piece measures 10" from beg of MC. Cut MC.

- Change to 1 strand each of CC1 and CC2 held tog. Sc 2 rnds. Cut CC2.

- With 1 strand of CC1, sc in both loops for 2 rnds. Fasten off.

- **Bottom trim:** With 1 strand each of CC1 and CC2 held tog, sc 1 rnd in free loops around bottom edge. Fasten off.

BUTTON FLAP

- Beg from marker, sk first 12 sts, attach 1 strand of MC in next st at center back and working in bls, sc in each of next 6 sts. Turn.

- Ch 1; working in bls, sc in first sc and in each sc across. Turn.

- Rep last row 7 more times.

- **Buttonhole row:** Ch 1, sc, ch 4, sk 4, sc. Turn.

- Ch 1; sc in first st, in each sc, and in each ch across. Fasten off.

POCKETS (MAKE 2)

- With 2 strands of CC1 held tog, ch 21. Sc in second ch from hook and in each ch across—20 sc. Turn.

- Work patt st until pocket measures 7". Fasten off.

FINISHING

- Felt bag and pockets according to instructions on page 12.

- Sew pockets to narrow ends of bag with matching embroidery floss.

- Sew handles to bag in 3 places with Super Suede as shown.

- Sew on button.

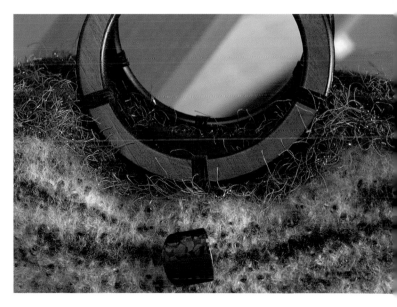

Lemon DROP

Small, sweet, and oh so cheerful, this little bit of sunshine would be the perfect bag for your little (or big) daughter or granddaughter.

Skill Level: Easy ◼◼◻◻

Finished Measurements after Felting
Approx 6" wide x 6½" high x 2" deep

MATERIALS

MC 1 skein of Cascade 220 from Cascade Yarns (100% wool; 100 g; 220 yds) in Quatro color 3612 Yellow

CC1 1 skein of Cascade 220 from Cascade Yarns in color 8505 White

CC2 1 skein of Fizz from Crystal Palace Yarns (100% polyester; 50 g; 120 yds) in color 7305 Sunshine [3]

K-10½ (6.5 mm) crochet hook

M-13 (9 mm) crochet hook

Stitch marker

2 large and 2 small flower-shaped buttons

Needle and thread

PATTERN STITCH

Row 1 (WS): Ch 1; working in fls, sc in first sc and in each sc across. Turn.

Row 2 (RS): Ch 1; working in bls, sc in first sc and in each sc across. Turn.

BAG

Beg bag at bottom. Unless otherwise instructed, use 1 strand of yarn throughout and work in bls only.

- With M hook and MC, ch 31. Sc in second ch from hook and in each ch across—30 sts. Turn.

- Ch 1, sc in first sc and in each sc across. Turn.

- Rep last row 7 more times.

- Turn piece 90° to right; work 7 sc in ends of rows, 30 sc in free loops of beg ch, 7 sc in opposite ends of rows—74 sts. Pm to mark beg of rnd.

- Working in bls, sc around until piece measures 8" from beg of rnds. Cut MC.

- Change to CC1 and sc 1 rnd.

- With K hook, sc 1 rnd. Cut CC1.

FLAP

- With RS facing you, M hook, and MC, attach yarn at marker. Working in bls, work 30 sc along back of bag. Turn.

- Work patt st until flap measures 3".

- **Buttonhole row:** Ch 1, sc in each of next 6 sc, ch 4, sk next 4 sc, sc in each of next 10 sc, ch 4, sk next 4 sc, sc in each of next 6 sc. Turn.

- Ch 1, sc in first st, in each sc, and in each ch across. Turn.

- Work patt st for 4 more rows. Fasten off.

HANDLES (MAKE 2)

- With M hook and MC, attach yarn at one corner of bag, working in bls, sc in each of next 7 sc across narrow end. Turn.

- Work patt st until handle measures 5" from beg.

- **Dec row:** Ch 1, sc2tog, sc in each of next 3 sc, sc2tog—5 sc. Turn.

- Work patt st until flap measures 10" from beg.

- **Dec row:** Ch 1, sc2tog, sc, sc2tog—3 sc. Turn.

- Work patt st until flap measures 15" from beg. Fasten off.

- Make second handle with CC1.

- With K hook and contrasting color, sc all around each handle.

TRIM

- For top, with RS facing you, with K hook and CC1, sc all around the top, working into free loops in front of base of flap and base of handles.

- For bottom, with RS facing you, with K hook and 1 strand each of CC1 and CC2 held tog, sc in free loops around flap and around bottom edge.

- For sides, with RS facing you, with M hook and CC1, beg from top of narrow end, sl st down one side, across bottom, and up other side. Rep at other end.

End here.

For sl st, start here.

FINISHING

- Felt bag according to instructions on page 12.

- Tie handles tog into a knot.

- Sew on buttons, placing small flower on top of large flower.

Lost HIPPIE

My friend Parrish gave me a look and asked, "Are you going to make one for us hippies?" A little "back to the future," with a pocket for a cell phone and an attached key chain.

Skill Level: Intermediate ◼◼◼◻

Finished Measurements after Felting
Approx 8" wide at bottom, 16" wide at middle x 12½" high

MATERIALS

Cascade 220 Heathers from Cascade Yarns (100% wool; 100 g; 220 yds) [4]

MC 3 skeins in Heather color 2424 Dark Denim

CC 1 skein in Heather color 2443 Light Sand

M 13 (9 mm) crochet hook

P-15 (10 mm) crochet hook

Stitch marker

10 large eyelets, 7/16" diameter

2 small eyelets, 1/4" diameter

6 pieces of leather lacing, each 1 yard long

1 yard of thin leather or suede yarn

Needle and embroidery floss

Small chain and hook for key chain

PATTERN STITCH

Row 1 (WS): Ch 1; working in fls, sc in first sc and in each sc across. Turn.

Row 2 (RS): Ch 1; working in bls, sc in first sc and in each sc across. Turn.

BAG

Beg bag at top. Unless otherwise instructed, use 1 strand of yarn throughout and work in bls only.

- With M hook and CC, ch 140, sl st to first ch to join into rnd, pm to mark beg of rnd.
- Sc around until piece measures 2½".
- **Inc rnd:** (Sc in each of next 13 sc, work 2 sc in next sc) around—150 sts. Cut CC.
- Change to P hook and MC. Sc around until piece measures 9" from inc rnd.
- **Dec rnd:** (Sc in each of next 13 sc, sc2tog) around—140 sts.
- Sc 6 rnds even.
- **Dec rnd:** (Sc in each of next 12 sc, sc2tog) around—130 sts.
- Sc 6 rnds even.
- **Dec rnd:** (Sc in each of next 11 sc, sc2tog) around—120 sts.
- Sc 2 rnds even.

- Work 4 more dec rnds, working 1 less st between dec—80 sts after fourth rnd.
- Sc 1 rnd even. Place second marker at st 41.
- Sc2tog, sc to 2 sts from next marker, sc2tog before and after marker, work to 2 sts from next marker, sc2tog.

  Rep last rnd 5 more times—56 sts. Fasten off. Leave tail for sewing up seam.

POCKET

- With M hook and CC, ch 21. Sc in second ch from hook and in each ch across—20 sts. Turn.
- Work patt st, inc 1 st at each end of next 5 rows—30 sts.
- Work patt st until piece measures 7". Cut CC.
- Change to MC and work patt st for another 1½" from beg of MC. Fasten off.

TRIM

With 2 strands of opposite color, whipstitch around top edge, on second row below MC on bag, and below CC on pocket. See page 15.

FINISHING

- Sew bottom seam.
- Felt bag and pocket according to instructions on page 12.
- Attach 5 large eyelets on front and 5 large eyelets on back, spacing them evenly around the top about 1/4" from edge.
- Attach 2 small eyelets to top corners of pocket. Sew pocket to front.
- Weave 3 strands of leather lacing through 5 eyelets on the front. Join ends tog, overlapping by about 2" and wrap ends with thin leather strip or suede yarn. Rep with 3 strands of leather lacing on back.
- Insert chain with hook into one of eyelets on pocket.

Violet HORIZON

The contrast between the delicate color and the rustic hobo shape gives this bag its charm. Think of a misty summer morning with dewdrops sparkling on the ground.

Skill Level: Easy ◖■□□

Finished Measurements after Felting
Approx 15½" at widest point x 11" high

MATERIALS

MC1 2 skeins of Cascade 220 from Cascade Yarns (100% wool; 100 g; 220 yds) in color 8912 Lavender (4)

MC2 3 skeins of Silk Garden Lite from Noro Yarns (45% silk, 45% kid mohair, 10% lamb's wool; 50 g; 136 yds) in color 2013 (3)

CC 1 skein of Gatsby from Katia (77% viscose, 15% nylon, 8% metallic polyester; 50 g; 129 yds) in color 34 (3)

M-13 (9 mm) crochet hook

Stitch markers

2 clear plastic O-rings, 1⅝" diameter

12"-long rhinestone zipper

1 package of Mill Hill Glass pebble beads

Optional: Chain and key ring; charm

Yarn needle

Sharp needle and thread for sewing zipper

BAG

Beg bag at top. Unless otherwise instructed, use 2 strands of yarn throughout and work in bls only.

- With 1 strand each of MC1 and MC2 held tog, ch 120, sl st to first ch to join into rnd. Pm in first st and in 61st st. Move markers up in each rnd.

- Sc 10 rnds.

- **Dec rnd:** *Sc2tog, sc to 2 sts from next marker, sc2tog before and after marker, sc to 2 sts from next marker, sc2tog.

- Sc 2 rnds even.*

- Rep from * to * 4 more times—100 sts.

- Sc2tog, sc to 2 sts from next marker, sc2tog before and after marker, sc to 2 sts from next marker, sc2tog.

- Rep last rnd 4 more times—80 sts.

- **Sc 1 rnd even.

- Sc2tog, sc to 2 sts from next marker, sc2tog before and after marker, sc to 2 sts from next marker, sc2tog.**

- Rep from ** to ** once more—72 sts. Fasten off.

- Sew bottom seam with 1 strand of MC1.

TOP TRIM

- With 1 strand each of MC1 and CC held tog, sc 1 rnd in free loops of beg ch. Cut CC.

- With 1 strand of MC1, working in both loops, sc 1 rnd. Fasten off.

HANDLE

- With 1 strand of MC1, ch 141. Sc in second ch from hook and in each ch across—140 sts. Turn.

- Ch 1, working in back loops, sc in first sc and in each sc across. Turn.

- Rep last row 2 more times.

FINISHING

- Using 2 strands of MC1, whipstitch O-rings to sides, working across 10 sts at end of bag.

- Loop handle through rings. Whipstitch ends of rows tog. Whipstitch edges of beg chain tog starting and ending 3" from each ring. Wrap yarn around open ends.

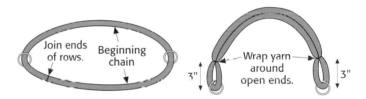

- Felt bag according to instructions on page 12.

- Sew in zipper (see page 15).

- With yarn needle and CC, work a running st along center of handle.

- With CC, make a tassel. String beads onto ties of tassel and attach to O-ring.

- Attach chain and key ring to O-ring if desired

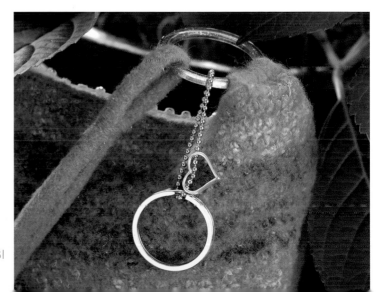

Patchwork

This slouchy, comfy hobo is designed to give you
a good feeling—the fall-is-here, harvesttime, back-to-school
kind of feeling. I am free!

Skill Level: Beginner ◼☐☐◻

Finished Measurements after Felting
Approx 17" wide at bottom x 9½" high at center

MATERIALS

Cascade 220 Heathers from Cascade Yarns (100% wool; 100 g; 220 yds) (4)

   A 2 skeins in color 2440 Rust

   B 1 skein in color 2437 Honey

   C 1 skein in color 8013 Brown

Small amount of Suede from Berroco (100% nylon; 50 g; 120 yds) in color 3717 for trim

M-13 (9 mm) crochet hook

2 plastic O-rings, 1⅝" diameter

20 flower eyelets

1 button, any size

Needle and pearl cotton

PATTERN STITCH

Row 1 (WS): Ch 1; working in fls, sc in first sc and in each sc across. Turn.

Row 2 (RS): Ch 1; working in bls, sc in first sc and in each sc across. Turn.

SIDE PANELS (MAKE 2)

Use 1 strand of yarn throughout.

- With A, ch 61. Sc in second ch from hook and in each ch across—60 sts. Turn.

- Work patt st until piece measures 4" from beg.

- Cont in patt st, sc2tog at each end of EOR 5 times—50 sts. Cut A.

- Change to B and work patt st for another 3".

- Cont in patt st, sc2tog at each end of EOR 5 times—40 sts.

- Work patt st for another 2". Fasten off.

CENTER PANELS (MAKE 2)

- With C, ch 31. Sc in second ch from hook and in each ch across—30 sts. Turn.

- Work patt st until panel measures 16".

JOIN PANELS

- With needle and yarn, whipstitch center panel to side panels (see page 15). Sew bottom seam, folding corners in approx 1".

- **Top edge:** Join B to beg of any panel; working in bl, sc 3 rnds. Fasten off.

HANDLES

- **Side handles:** *Mark center 20 sts of joined side panel. With RS facing, join C to first st on top edge. Work patt st until handle measures 5" from beg.

   Dec row: Cont patt st, sc2tog at each end—18 sts.

   Cont patt st until handle measures 8" from beg.

   Dec row: Cont patt st, sc2tog at each end—16 sts.

   Cont patt st until handle measures 10" from beg. Fasten off.

   Rep from * for second handle at opposite side panel.

- **Middle handle:** With A, ch 15. Sc in second ch from hook and in each sc across—14 sts. Turn. Work patt st until piece measures 13". Fasten off.

FINISHING

- Fold handle ends over O-rings and sew tog with 1 strand of matching yarn.

- Felt bag according to instructions on page 12.

- Attach 5 eyelets each to top of side panels on front and back.

- Using pearl cotton, work a running stitch around 3 sides of both B-colored blocks. Whipstitch a strand of Suede around the running stitch.

- Whipstitch 1 strand of Suede around edges of handles and along top edge of bag. See page 15.

- For tie, cut 2 strands of Suede, 32" long. Fold in half and make a twisted cord. Attach to middle of center panel on one side of bag.

- Sew a button on opposite center panel. Twist cord around button to close bag.

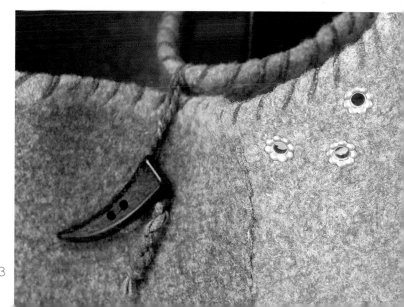

A TISKET, a Tasket

Don't let the sweet look fool you. This bag can hold a lot of stuff.
It opens wide so you can see what's inside.

Skill Level: Experienced ◖■■▶

Finished Measurements after Felting
Approx 15" wide at top x 7½" high x 3" deep

MATERIALS

Cascade 220 from Cascade Yarns (100% wool; 100 g; 220 yds) (**4**)

    MC 2 skeins in color 8401 Grey

    CC 1 skein in color 8913 Pink

K-10½ (6.5 mm) crochet hook

M-13 (9 mm) crochet hook

P-15 (10 mm) crochet hook

Stitch markers

2 pieces of 10-mm diameter vinyl tubing for handles, 19" long

2 bead clasps

4 charms

Sewing thread and sharp needle

BAG

Beg bag at bottom. Work in bls only unless otherwise instructed.

- With P hook and 2 strands of MC, ch 26. Sc in second ch from hook and in each ch across to last ch, work 2 sc in last ch, pm; working on opposite side, sc in free loops of beg ch to last ch, work 2 sc in last ch, pm—51 sts.

- (Sc to marker, work 2 sc in marked st) twice.

- Rep last row once more—55 sts.

- (Sc to 1 st before marker, work 2 sc in each of next 4 sc) twice.

- Rep last row once more—63 sts.

- Sc 3 rnds. Cut 1 strand of MC.

- With M hook and 1 strand of MC, work 2 dc in each sc around—126 sts.

- Work patt sequence as follows:

   Rnd 1: Sc in first dc and in each dc around.

   Rnd 2: Ch 2 (counts as 1 dc), dc in each sc, sl st to top of beg ch.

   Rep last 2 rnds 6 more times.

   Work rnd 1 once more. Cut MC.

- Change to 1 strand of CC. Sc 5 rnds.

- With K hook and working in fls, sc 1 rnd. Fasten off.

FLAPS (MAKE 2)

- Mark center 23 sts on front of bag. With RS facing you, M hook, and 1 strand of CC, attach yarn in first st and work row 1 across 23 sts

- **Row 1 (RS):** Ch 1; working in bls, sc in first sc and in each sc across. Turn.

   Row 2: Ch 1, working in fls, sc in first sc and in each sc across. Turn.

   Rep rows 1 and 2 until flap measures 2½". Fasten off.

- Make second flap on back.

BASKET WEAVE PATTERN

- With M hook and 1 strand of MC, ch 100 loosely. Fasten off. Make 7 pieces.

- On dc rnds only, beg at one side, weave chain under 1 dc and over 3 dc all around. Join and secure ends inside bag.

HANDLES (MAKE 2)

- With M hook and 1 strand of CC, ch 8. Sc in second ch from hook and in each ch across—7 sts. Turn.

- **Row 1 (WS):** Ch 1; working in fls, sc in first sc and in each sc across. Turn.

   Row 2: Ch 1; working in bls, sc in first sc and in each sc across. Turn.

   Rep rows 1 and 2 until handle measures 21".

- Fold handle in half lengthwise. Whipstitch edges tog, beg approx 2" from one end and ending 2" from opposite end.

- Slide vinyl tubing inside. Tack ends with sewing thread and sharp needle through tubing several times. After the wool felts, it leaves a netlike texture.

FINISHING

- Felt bag and handles according to instructions on page 12.

- Flatten handle ends and cut into heart shape. Sew heart ends of handles to front and back of bag.

- Sew clasps to flaps.

- Sew charms on top of heart-shaped handle ends.

Plum PASSION

You can fall in love with the color, the shape, the cute
handles—or you can just fall in love.

Skill Level: Intermediate ◼◼◼◻

Finished Measurements after Felting
Approx 11" wide x 10" high at sides x 3" deep

MATERIALS

Cascade 220 from Cascade Yarns (100% wool; 100 g; 220 yds)

MC 2 skeins in color 8886 Plum

CC 1 skein In color 8912 Violet

Small amount of Suede from Berroco (100% nylon; 50 g; 120 yds) in color 3755 for sewing handle

M-13 (9 mm) crochet hook

1 pair of coffee-colored round rattan handles, 7½" diameter

2 small magnetic snaps

3 buttons, ½" diameter

Hole puncher

1 Clover Needle Felting Tool Kit

Needle and thread for sewing

PATTERN STITCH

Row 1 (WS): Ch 1; working in fls, sc in first sc and in each sc across. Turn.

Row 2 (RS): Ch 1; working in bls, sc in first sc and in each sc across. Turn.

BAG

Use 1 strand of yarn throughout.

FRONT AND BACK PANEL (MAKE 2)

Work in patt st throughout front and back panels.

- With MC, ch 51. Sc in second ch from hook and in each ch across—50 sts. Turn.

- Work patt st until piece measures 12".

- **Shape first side:** With RS facing you, sc in each of next 15 sc. Turn.

  Dec row: Ch 1, sc2tog, sc in each sc across. Turn.

  Rep dec row EOR a total of 3 times—12 sts.

  Work 4 rows even. Fasten off.

- **Shape second side:** With RS facing you, sk center 20 sc, join yarn in next sc, and sc in each of next 15 sc. Turn.

  Dec row: Ch 1, sc in first st and in each sc across to last 2 sts, sc2tog.

Rep dec row EOR a total of 3 times—12 sts.

Work 4 rows even. Fasten off.

- With RS facing you, join MC to top left corner, dc around panels as follows: work 48 dc in ends of rows, 50 dc in free loops of beg ch, and 48 dc in opposite ends of rows. Fasten off.

GUSSET

- With RS facing you, join CC to 13th st from top left corner of back panel. Working in bls, sc down one side, across bottom, and up other side, ending 12 sts before end of panel.

- Work 12 rows in patt st. Do not cut CC.

- **Join gusset and front panel:** With WS tog, beg in 13th st of front panel; with front panel facing you, sc in bls of CC and fls of MC. At end, do not turn. Work reverse sc (see page 14) in bls of joining row. This creates a miniruffle. Fasten off. Work 1 row of reverse sc on back panel as well.

POCKET

- With MC, ch 27, sc in second ch from hook and in each ch across—26 sts. Turn.

- Work patt st until pocket measures 6". Fasten off.

- Following instructions on needle felting tool kit, make 3 circles with CC on pocket.

FINISHING

- Felt bag and pocket according to instructions on page 12.

- Punch holes evenly around curved portion of top to match spaces on handle. Sew handle to top with Suede.

- Sew pocket to front.

- Attach magnetic snaps to top corners of front and back. Sew button on top to cover snaps.

- Sew button on pocket.

CAFÉ au Lait

This is a perfect basket to take to the market.
Enjoy a cup of coffee while you shop.

Skill Level: Intermediate ◼◼◼◻

Finished Measurements after Felting
Approx 12" wide at bottom, 17" wide at top x 9" high x 3" deep

MATERIALS

Cascade 220 from Cascade Yarns (100% wool; 100 g; 220 yds) (4)

MC 2 skeins in color 8021 Beige

CC1 1 skein in color 8622 Light Brown

CC2 1 skein in color 8010 Cream

Small amount of Suede from Berroco (100% nylon; 50 g; 120 yds) in color 3714 Brown for trim

K-10½ (6.5 mm) crochet hook

M-13 (9 mm) crochet hook

P-15 (10 mm) crochet hook

Stitch markers

1 pair of rattan handles, 9¾" wide x 8¾" high

Assortment of wooden beads

Tapestry needle, embroidery needle, and pearl cotton for sewing the pocket

BAG

Beg bag at bottom. Use 2 strands of yarn throughout unless otherwise instructed. Work in bls only unless otherwise instructed.

- With P hook and CC1, ch 37. Sc in second ch from hook and in each ch across to last ch, work 3 sc in last ch. Do not turn. Working along opposite side, sc in free loops of beg ch to last ch, work 2 sc in last ch—74 sts. Pm in last st and in 37th st. Move markers up each rnd, placing them on middle st of 3 sc.

- **Inc rnd:** Sc around, working 3 sc in each marked st—78 sts.

- Rep last rnd 2 more times—86 sts.

- Ch 2 (counts as 1 dc), dc in each st around. Sl st to top of beg ch 2.

- Sc 1 rnd. Cut CC1.

- Change to MC. Work patt sequence as follows:

  1 rnd sc, 1 rnd dc, 1 rnd sc, rep from * to * a total of 4 times.

- **Inc rnd:** Mark first and 44th st, move markers up each rnd. **Sc to marker, work 2 sc in marked st, rep from ** to end of rnd—88 sts.

- Rep inc rnd 4 more times—96 sts.

- Sc 1 rnd. Cut MC.

- Change to CC2. Sc 2 rnds.

- Working in both loops, sc 1 rnd. Fasten off.

BOTTOM TRIM

With M hook and 2 strands of MC, sc 1 rnd in free loops around bottom edge.

TIES (MAKE 4)

- With K hook and 1 strand of CC1, ch 31. Sc in second ch from hook and in each ch across—30 sts. Fasten off.

- Attach loops under top row of bag approx 6" from each end on front and back. Fold tie in half, push through from front to back and flip tails through loop.

POCKET

- With M hook and 1 strand of CC1, ch 41. Sc in second ch from hook and in each ch across—40 sts.

  Row 1: Ch 1, sc in first st and in each st across. Turn.

  Row 2: Ch 2 (count as dc), dc in each sc across. Turn.

  Work rows 1 and 2 another 3 times.

  Rep row 1 once more. Cut CC1.

- Change to CC2 and K hook. Ch 1; working in both loops, sc in first sc and in each sc across. Fasten off.

FINISHING

- Felt bag and pocket according to instructions on page 12.

- Whipstitch pocket inside bag, aligning bottom of pocket with bottom of bag.

- Sew beads to front with Suede.

- Attach handles to ties with a square knot.

- Whipstitch around top with Suede. See page 15.

Lime SHERBET

Fresh and cool, but sweet at the same time.
The beads in icy watercolors add to the refreshing charm of this bag.

Skill Level: Easy ◼◼☐◻

Finished Measurements after Felting
Approx 12" wide x 8½" high x 3" deep

MATERIALS

Cascade 220 Quatro from Cascade Yarns (100% wool; 100 g; 220 yds) (**4**)

MC 2 skeins in color 5019 Light Green

CC 1 skein in color 2448 Teal Heather

M-13 (9 mm) crochet hook

Stitch marker

1 pair of bamboo handles, 12" long

Assortment of acrylic beads

1 button, 1¼" diameter (from Gita Maria)

Needle and embroidery floss to match MC and CC

PATTERN STITCH

Row 1 (RS): Ch 1; working in bls, sc in first sc and in each sc across. Turn.

Row 2 (WS): Ch 1; working in fls, sc in first sc and in each sc across. Turn.

BAG

Beg bag at bottom. Use 1 strand of yarn throughout unless otherwise instructed.

- With CC, ch 51, sc in second ch from hook and in each ch across   50 sts. Turn.

- Ch 1; working in both loops, sc in first st and in each sc across. Turn.

- Rep last row 11 more times.

- Turn work 90° to right; work 10 sc in ends of rows, 50 sc in free loops of beg ch, 10 sc in opposite ends of rows—120 sts. Cut CC.

- Change to MC, pm to mark beg of rnd. Working in bls, sc around until piece measures 10" from beg of MC.

- **Pocket opening:** Sc in each of next 10 sc, ch 30, sk 30, sc to end of rnd. Sc in each sc and in each ch around.

- Working in bls, sc around for another 2".

- **Top edge:** Add CC, (sc 1 st in MC, sc 1 st in CC) around. Cut MC.

- With CC, (working in bls, sc in each of next 50 sc; working in both loops, sc in each of next 10 sc) twice.

HANDLES

- **Front handles:** *Work patt st on 50 sts for 2", ending with WS row.

- Working in first 14 sts, work patt st for 5". Fasten off.

- With RS facing you, sk center 22 sts; join yarn in next st and work patt st on 14 sts for 5". Fasten off.*

- **Back handles:** From left side of front handle section, skip next 10 sts. Join yarn in next st and work from * to * on next 50 sts.

- With RS facing you and working in bls, sc around top and handles.

POCKET LINING

With RS facing you and holding bag with bottom up, join MC to first free loop of pocket ch. Work patt st until pocket measures 8". Fasten off.

TRIM

- **For pocket:** Weave 3 strands of CC across top (over 1 st, under 1 st), leaving 7" tails at each end to string beads. Tie a knot at *base* of tails.

- **For bottom:** With 1 strand of MC, sc 1 rnd in free loops around bottom edge.

FINISHING

- Felt bag according to instructions on page 12.

- Sew pocket lining inside bag.

- Fold handle flaps over bamboo sticks and sew ends to handle.

- String assorted beads onto yarn tails and knot ends.

BLUE Moon

Simple elegance describes this bag best. The flap sparkles with every move when the crystal beads catch the light.

Skill Level: Easy ◖■☐◗

Finished Measurements after Felting
Approx 11" wide x 8" high x 2" deep

MATERIALS

MC 5 skeins of Julia from Nashua Handknits (50% wool, 25% alpaca, 25% kid mohair; 50 g; 93 yds) in color 6396 Deep Blue Sea **4**

CC 1 skein of New Smoking from Filatura di Crosa (65% viscose, 35% polyamide; 25 g; 132 yds) in color 5 Blue **3**

K-10½ (6.5 mm) crochet hook

M-13 (9 mm) crochet hook

Stitch marker

2 purse clamps and snaps

12 beads from Mill Hill Crystal Treasures, color 13069

1 button, 1½" diameter

Tapestry needle

PATTERN STITCH

Row 1 (WS): Ch1; working in fls, sc in first sc and in each sc across. Turn.

Row 2 (RS): Ch 1; working in bls, sc in first sc and in each sc across. Turn.

BAG

Beg bag at bottom. Use 1 strand of yarn throughout unless otherwise instructed.

- With M hook and MC, ch 41. Sc in second ch from hook and in each ch across—40 sts. Turn.

- Work patt st until piece measures 4", ending with RS row.

- Turn piece 90° to right; work 2 sc in corner, 11 sc in ends of rows, 2 sc in corner, 40 sc in free loops of beg ch, 2 sc in corner, 11 sc in opposite end rows, 2 sc in corner—110 sts. Pm to mark beg of rnd.

- Working in bls, sc around until piece measures 10" from beg of rnds.

- With K hook and working in fls, sc 2 rnds. Do not fasten off.

FLAP

- Add 1 strand of CC to MC. With M hook, work next 40 sts in patt st until flap measures 4½".

- Cont in patt st, sc2tog twice at each end of next 9 rows—4 sts. Cut CC.

- **Buttonhole row:** Cont with MC, sl st in first sc, ch 8, sk 2 sc, sl st in last sc. Fasten off.

- Work 1 row of sc around flap, working 8 sc in ch-8 sp.

HANDLE TABS

- With RS facing you, join MC in third st to left of flap. Sc in each of next 11 sts.

- Work patt st for 7 rows. Fasten off.

- For opposite tab, with RS facing you, join yarn in 14th st to right of flap. Working back toward flap, sc in each of next 11 sts. Work pattern st for 7 rows. Fasten off.

HANDLE

- With M hook and MC, ch 13. Sc in second ch from hook and in each ch across—12 sts.

- Work patt st until handle measures 18". Fasten off.

FINISHING

- Felt bag and handle according to instructions on page 12.

- With tapestry needle and CC, sew ch-st swirls on top of flap (see page 15). Sew beads in clusters of 3 into design.

- Attach clamp to handle. Attach snaps to handle tabs. Fold ends of tab over and tack in place to cover back of snap.

- Sew on button.

Starburst

G Golden rays seem to be shooting out of the corner.
This elegant evening bag sure could keep up with the stars.

Skill Level: Beginner ◖☐☐▷

Finished Measurements after Felting
Approx 10" wide x 8" high

MATERIALS

MC 2 skeins of Cascade 220 from Cascade Yarns (100% wool; 100 g; 220 yds) in color 2401 Burgundy (4)

CC 1 skein of New Smoking from Filatura di Crosa (65% viscose, 35% polyester; 25 g; 132 yds) in color 1 Gold (3)

K-10½ (6.5 mm) crochet hook

M-13 (9 mm) crochet hook

½ yard of gold/burgundy beaded trim

1 magnetic snap

1 button, ¾" diameter

Needle and sewing thread to match MC

PATTERN STITCH

Row 1 (WS): Ch 1; working in fls, sc in first sc and in each sc across. Turn.

Row 2 (RS): Ch 1; working in bls, sc in first sc and in each sc across. Turn.

BAG

Bag is worked flat. Use 1 strand of yarn throughout.

- With M hook and MC, ch 45. Sc in second ch from hook and in each ch across—44 sts. Turn.

- Work patt st until piece measures 19", ending with WS row. Turn. Drop, but do not cut MC.

FLAP

- With RS facing, join CC. Ch 1; working in bls, sc in first st and in each sc across. Cut CC. Go back to beg of row, and with MC, work 2 more rows in patt st.

- Shape flap as follows:

  Row 1: Ch 1, sc2tog, work row 1 of patt st to end of row. Turn.

  Row 2: Work row 2 of patt st to last 2 sts, sc2tog. Turn.

  Rep rows 1 and 2 until 17 sts rem. Fasten off.

EDGING

With RS facing you and K hook, attach MC to beg ch. Sc in free loops of beg ch (this will become front edge), in ends of rows, and in sts all around, then once more across top front edge.

HANDLE

- With M hook and MC, ch 90. Sc in second ch from hook and in each ch across to last ch, work 2 sc in next ch; working along opposite side, sc in free loops of beg ch to last ch, work 2 sc in last ch. Fasten off.

- With CC, whipstitch around both sides and ends of handle (see page 15).

FINISHING

- Whipstitch around flap with CC (see page 15).

- Felt bag and handle according to instructions on page 12.

- Sew bead trim to each side on WS of top half of bag as shown. With WS facing tog, fold bag in half and sew sides tog, leaving beads outside.

- Sew handles to sides with CC.

- Attach magnetic snap. Sew button on top to cover prongs.

- With CC, work running stitch in rays on flap (see photo on facing page).

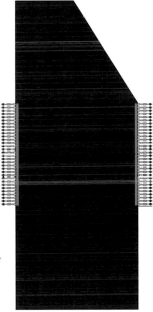

Heartfelt

This sweet little bag is transformed into a clutch
when the handle is removed—not your everyday felted bag.
You just have to love it.

Skill Level: Beginner ◼☐☐☐

Finished Measurements after Felting
Approx 10½" wide x 6" high

MATERIALS

MC 1 skein of Cascade 220 from Cascade Yarns (100% wool; 100 g; 220 yds) in color 8895 Red 4

CC1 1 skein of New Smoking from Filatura di Crosa (65% viscose, 35% polyester; 25 g; 132 yds) in color 6 Red 3

CC2 1 skein of Touch Me from Muench Yarns (72% rayon, 28% wool; 50 g; 132 yds) in color 3600 Red 4

H-8 (5 mm) crochet hook

M-13 (9 mm) crochet hook

Stitch marker

1 magnetic snap

2 red snaps

1 heart button, 1¼"-high (from Gita Maria)

PATTERN STITCH

Row 1 (WS): Ch 1; working in fls, sc in first sc and in each sc across. Turn.

Row 2 (RS): Ch 1; working in bls, sc in first sc and in each sc across. Turn.

BAG

Beg bag at bottom. Unless otherwise instructed, use 1 strand of yarn throughout and work in bls only.

- With M hook and MC, ch 86. Join with sl st to beg ch. Pm to mark beg of rnd.
- Sc around until piece measures 9". Do not cut yarn.

FLAP

- Sl st in each of next 5 sc. Working in bls, sc in each of next 33 sc. Turn.
- Add CC1 to MC and work patt st until flap measures 4".

- **Shape flap:** Sl st in first 5 sc, work patt st to last 5 sc—23 sts. Turn.
- Rep last row once more—13 sts. Turn.
- Ch 1, sc in first sc and in each sc across. Fasten off.
- With H hook and CC2, sc around flap and across top of front.

HANDLE

- With M hook and MC, ch 81. Sc in second ch from hook and in each ch across—80 sts. Turn. Fasten off.
- With H hook and CC2, ch 1. Working in bls, sc in first sc and in each sc across; working along opposite side, sc in free loops of beg ch to end. Fasten off.

FINISHING

- Sew bottom seam, making small pleat in each corner.
- Felt bag and handle according to instructions on page 12.
- Attach red snaps to handle and to sides of bag.
- Attach magnetic snap on front flap. Sew on button to cover prongs.

Little Brown BAG

Whether you're "brown bagging" or going out to lunch, this tailored bag means business.

Skill Level: Intermediate ◖◼◼◗▢

Finished Measurements after Felting
Approx 11½" wide x 8" high x 2" deep

MATERIALS

Cascade 220 from Cascade Yarns (100% wool; 100 g; 220 yds) ④

    MC 3 skeins in Heather color 8012 Light Brown

    CC 1 skein in color 7824 Orange

K-10½ (6.5 mm) crochet hook

M-13 (9 mm) crochet hook

Stitch marker

4 heavy-duty silver snaps

2 enamel buckles, 1¼" square

4 small eyelets

Needle and embroidery floss to match MC to sew pocket linings in place

PATTERN STITCH

Row 1 (WS): Ch 1; working in fls, sc in first sc and in each sc across. Turn.

Row 2 (RS): Ch 1; working in bls, sc in first sc and in each sc across. Turn.

BAG

Beg bag at bottom. Use 1 strand of yarn throughout. Work in bls only unless otherwise instructed.

- With M hook and MC, ch 120, sl st to beg ch to join into rnd, pm to mark beg of rnd.
- Sc around until piece measures 9½" from beg.
- **Pocket openings:** Sc in each of next 8 sc, ch 17, sk next 17 sc, sc in each of next 10 sc, ch 17, sk next 17 sc, sc to end of rnd. Sc in each sc and in each ch around.
- Sc around until piece measures 15½" from beg.
- Working in both loops with K hook and CC, sc 1 rnd. Fasten off.

FLAP

- With WS facing you, M hook, and MC, join yarn to sixth st from marker, toward back of bag. Work patt st over next 50 sts until flap measures 4".
- Ch 1, sc2tog, work in patt st to last 2 sc, sc2tog—48 sts.
- Rep last row 2 more times—44 sts. Fasten off.

POCKET LININGS (MAKE 2)

- With WS facing you, join MC to first ch of pocket opening, work 2 sc in same st, sc in each of next 15 sc, work 2 sc in last st—19 sts.
- Work patt st until pocket measures 7½". Fasten off.

SIDE STRAPS AND HANDLE

- **Side straps (make 2):** With M hook and CC, ch 31. Sc in second ch from hook and in each ch to last ch, work 2 sc in last ch; working along opposite side, sc in free loops of beg ch to last ch, work 2 sc in last sc. Sc 1 rnd. Fasten off.
- **Handle (make 1):** Ch 101. Work as for side straps.

FINISHING

- With MC, whipstitch all around edges of straps, and handle (see page 15).
- **Pocket and flap trims:** With RS facing you, K hook, and CC, sc 1 row across front pocket openings and around flap.
- Sew bottom seam.
- Sew side straps under bottom corners, overlapping corner by about 2".
- Felt bag and handle according to instructions on page 12.
- Sew pocket linings in place.
- Attach snaps to flap, sides, and side straps.
- Cut 1¼"-wide slits on each side at pocket level and then 1" from top. Lace side straps through slits and attach buckle. Attach eyelets to handle 3" from ends. Buckle up.

Mardi GRAS

Bright colors, funky fringes, and beads look like a fun time,
so you might want to take this tote to a concert or a parade.
Colorful pockets for accessories are a plus.

Skill Level: Intermediate ■■■□

Finished Measurements after Felting
Approx 13" wide x 10½" high x 5" deep

MATERIALS

Cascade 220 from Cascade Yarns (100% wool; 100 g; 220 yds) (4)

MC 3 skeins in color 8555 Black

CC1 1 skein in color 2409 Green

CC2 1 skein in color 7826 Orangey Yellow

CC3 1 skein in color 7803 Magenta

CC4 1 skein of Kureyon from Noro (100% wool; 50 g; 109 yds) in color 154 (4)

M-13 (9 mm) crochet hook

Stitch marker

Assortment of colored wooden beads

Tapestry needle and embroidery floss

PATTERN STITCH

Row 1 (WS): Ch 1; working in fls, sc in first sc and in each sc across. Turn.

Row 2 (RS): Ch 1; working in bls, sc in first sc and in each sc across. Turn.

BAG

Beg bag at bottom. Use 1 strand of yarn unless otherwise instructed.

- With CC1, ch 51. Sc in second ch from hook and in each ch across—50 sts. Turn.

- Ch 1; working in bls, sc in first st and in each sc across. Turn.

- Work last row 13 more times. Do not turn at end of last row.

- With RS facing you, turn bottom 90° to right; work 15 sc in ends of rows, 50 sc in free loops of beg ch, 15 sc in opposite ends of rows—130 sts. Pm to mark beg of rnd. Cut CC1.

- Change to CC2; sc in bls for 1 rnd, working 3 sc in each corner st (50th, 65th, 115th, and 130th st)—138 sts. Cut CC2. Pm in middle st of 3 sc corner st, using different color marker to indicate beg of rnd.

- Change to CC3; sc in bls for 1 rnd, working 3 sc in each marked st—146 sts. Cut CC3. You can remove markers after this rnd or move them up each rnd to help you remember when to switch from dc to sc.

- Change to MC. Work patt as follows:

  Rnd 1: Working in bls, sc around.

  Rnd 2: Working in bls, (dc in each of next 54 sc, sc in each of next 19 sc) twice.

  Work rnds 1 and 2 another 13 times (total of 14 dc rows on each side).

  Work rnd 1 once more.

- Working in bls, sc 1 rnd each with CC3, CC2, and CC1. Fasten off.

- Working on dc portion of each side, weave CC4 as follows: Beg at bottom of bag in first dc row, work from right to left, under 1 dc and over 1 dc across, then back across, under 1 dc and over 1 dc, on next dc row. Knot ends, leaving approx 3" tails. For next 2 dc rows, start at opposite end and work from left to right and then back again. Alternate start of weaving every 2 rows.

BOTTOM TRIM

With MC, sc 1 rnd in free loops around bottom edge.

HANDLES

- From each of CC1, CC2, and CC3, cut 6 strands, each 3 yds long.

- Using 6 strands from each of 3 colors, make a knot at one end, leaving a 3" tail. Braid 3 colors to opposite end and tie a knot, leaving a 3" tail.

- Cut braided handle in half to make 2 handles. Tie a knot in cut ends, leaving 3" tails at each end.

- Stitch each end of a handle to the top 8 sts at each end. Whipstitch around ends where handle is attached to bag to secure.

POCKETS (MAKE 2)

- With CC2, ch 21, sc in second ch from hook and in each sc across—20 sts.

- Work patt st until pocket measures 8". Fasten off.

- Make second pocket with CC3.

FINISHING

- Felt bag according to instructions on page 12.

- Sew pockets to narrow ends of bag.

- String beads to ends of tails; tie a knot to secure bead. Note that sometimes the yarns stick together, but you can separate them by pulling them apart.

Career CASUAL

A perfect size for laptop, notes, or books, this bag has a large inside pocket to keep things organized. A little glitter blended into the yarn gives this roomy tote a special touch of class.

Skill Level: Easy ◀■□□

Finished Measurements after Felting
Approx 14" wide x 11½" high x 4¼" deep

MATERIALS

Cascade 220 from Cascade Yarns (100% wool; 100 g; 220 yds) 🔳4

   MC1 3 skeins in color 9447 Green

   CC1 1 skein in color 8885 Purple

   CC2 1 skein in color 2415 Mustard

   MC2 4 skeins of Aurora from Noro (55% wool, 20% kid mohair, 20% silk, 5% polyester; 40 g; 104 m) in color 3 🔳3

K-10½ (6.5 mm) crochet hook

M-13 (9 mm) crochet hook

Stitch marker

4 D rings, ¾"

4 large purse bottoms. These are brads that protect the bottom of the bag.

1 magnetic snap

1 button, 1½" diameter

Embroidery needle and pearl cotton

BAG

Beg bag at bottom.

- With M hook and 2 strands of CC1, ch 51. Sc in second ch from hook and in each ch across—50 sts. Turn.

- Ch 1; working in bls, sc in first sc and in each sc across. Turn.

- Rep last row until piece measures 6". Do not turn after last row.

- With RS facing you, turn work 90° to right; work 15 sc in end of rows, 50 sc in free loops of beg ch, 15 sc in opposite end of rows—130 sts. Pm to mark beg of rnd. Cut CC1.

- Change to 1 strand each of MC1 and MC2 held tog. Working in both loops, sc 1 rnd.

- Working in bls, sc around until piece measures 12" from beg of MC1 and MC2. Cut MC2.

- With 1 strand of MC1, sc 4 rnds. Cut MC1.

- Change to CC1, sc 1 rnd. Cut CC1.

FLAP

- With 2 strands of MC1, starting 5 sts before marker, working in bls, sc in each of next 60 sc. Cut 1 strand of MC1.

- Ch 1; working in both loops, sc in first st and in each sc across. Turn—60 sts.

- Rep last row until flap measures 4".

- **Dec row:** Ch 1, sc2tog, working in bls, sc in each sc to last 2 sts, sc2tog. Turn.

- Rep last row 7 more times—44 sts.

- Ch 1, sc in first sc and in each sc across. Turn.

- Rep last row once more. Fasten off.

- With 2 strands of MC1, and working in both loops, sc around flap. Fasten off.

HANDLES (MAKE 2)

- With M hook and 1 strand of MC1, ch 71 loosely. Sc in second ch from hook and in each ch across—70 sts. Turn.

- Ch 1; working in bls, sc in first sc and in each sc across. Turn. Cut MC1. Change to 1 strand of CC2.

- Ch 1; working in fls, sc in first sc and in each sc across. Turn.

- Rep last rnd once more. Fasten off.

- Fold each end over D ring and sew in place with yarn.

STRAPS (MAKE 4)

- With K hook and 1 strand of CC2, ch 7. Sc in second loop from hook and in each ch across—6 sts. Turn.

- Ch 1; working in both loops, sc in first st and in each sc across. Turn.

- Rep last row until piece measures 11". Fasten off.

- Fold 1 end of strap over D ring and sew in place with yarn.

POCKET

- With M hook and 1 strand of CC2, ch 51. Sc in second ch from hook and in each ch across—50 sts.

- Ch 1; working both loops, sc in first sc and in each sc across. Turn.

- Rep last row until pocket measures 10". Cut CC2.

- With MC1, sc 1 row. Fasten off.

FINISHING

- With 2 strands of CC1 held tog, sc 1 rnd in free loops around bottom edge.

- Felt bag, straps, handles, and pocket according to instructions on page 12.

- Position straps approx 2½" from each side and even with bottom edge (see photo on page 52). Using pearl cotton and beg at bottom, sew down center of each strap and then backstitch across top just below opening for D ring.

- Sew pocket inside bag.

- Attach magnetic snap. Sew button on flap to cover back of snap.

- Insert prongs on purse bottoms through bottom fabric of bag from outside to inside, and bend the prongs flat on the inside of the bag. Attach 4 purse bottoms, one approx 1" from each corner on bottom of bag.

Anything You Want It to Be

Multipurpose, multidirectional, multicolor—anything goes.
This bag is definitely fun, and with inside pockets, it's also functional.
Make it your own masterpiece.

Skill Level: Intermediate ◼◼◼◻

Finished Measurements after Felting
Approx 15" wide x 11" high x 4½" deep

MATERIALS

MC 2 skeins of Cascade 220 from Cascade Yarns (100% wool; 100 g; 220 yds) in color 2403 Dark Brown **(4)**

CC Approx 660 yds in assorted colors of Cascade 220 or other worsted-weight yarn and novelty yarns

K-10½ (6.5 mm) crochet hook

M-13 (9 mm) crochet hook

1 pair of purse handles, 2" x 27" (Brown Croc from Leisure Arts)

12"-long zipper for inside pocket

Embellishments of your choice

Clover Needle Felting Tool Kit (optional)

Tapestry needle and embroidery floss

PATTERN STITCH

Row 1 (WS): Ch 1; working in fls, sc in first st and in each st across. Turn.

Row 2 (RS): Ch 1; working in bls, sc in first st and in each st across. Turn.

BAG FRONT AND BACK

Bag is worked from center, free-form fashion, in multiple directions. Use 1 strand of worsted-weight yarn throughout. Do not use novelty yarns alone. Always combine 1 strand of novelty yarn with 1 strand of wool and work them together.

- *With M hook and using desired color, ch 21, sc in second ch from hook and in each ch across—20 sts. Turn.

- Work patt st for 4". Cut first color.

- Change color, and with RS facing you, turn piece 90° to right; sc across end of rows, picking up 1 st in each row. Work patt st for 2".

- Turn 90° to right; join new color at corner st and sc across to other end, working in ends of rows, in free loops of beg ch, or in back loops of sts. Work patt st to desired width or until color runs out.

After finishing each segment, you can continue to turn the piece 90° to the right with the right side facing you, going around and around the center section. Or you can join yarn at another end and work in another direction, but always join yarn with right side facing you. Work segments in pattern stitch to desired width. If you want to continue the same color for the next segment, make sure you end with a right-side row, turn the piece, and using the same color, work into stitches along the adjacent edge. Continue turning and adding segments until panel measures approx 24" wide x 19" high. You may need to work wider segments at the sides and narrower segments at the top and bottom to reach the desired size.

- When panel measures about 24" x 19", join MC to top left corner of long end of panel; work 50 sc in side, 60 sc in bottom, and 50 sc in opposite side.* Fasten off. Note that if your panel is a different size, you will need to adjust the number of sts that you work along the sides and bottom edge. Fasten off.

- Rep from * to * for second panel. **Do not fasten off.**

GUSSET

- Cont with MC and M hook, work patt st around sides and along bottom until gusset measures 8".

- **Join panels:** Holding gusset and rem panel with WS tog, sc in bls of gusset and in fls of panel.

TOP TRIM

- Working in both loops with M hook and MC, work 20 sc along end of gusset, 60 sc along top of panel, 20 sc along other end of gusset, and 60 sc along second panel—160 sts.

- Working in bls, sc 6 rnds.

- Change to K hook. Working in bls, sc 2 rnds. Fasten off.

FLAP

- Mark center 20 sts in back of bag. Working in third row from top on RS with M hook and MC, sc in each of 20 sts. Turn.

- Work patt st until flap measures 7".

- Ch 1, sc2tog, sc in each sc across to last 2 sts, sc2tog—18 sts. Turn.

- Rep last row 3 more times—12 sts. Fasten off.

POCKETS

- **Small inside pockets (make 2):** With desired color, ch 25. Sc in second ch from hook and in each ch across—24 sts. Turn.

  Work patt st until pocket measures 8". Fasten off.

- **Large zipper pocket:** With desired color, ch 51. Sc in second ch from hook and in each ch across—50 sts. Turn.

  Work patt st until pocket measures 8".

- **Zipper opening:** Ch 1, sc in first sc and in each of next 5 sc, ch 38, sk 38, work 6 sc. Turn. Ch 1, sc in first sc and in each sc and each ch across. Turn.

  Work 3 rows in patt st. Fasten off.

FINISHING

- Felt bag and pockets according to instructions on page 12.

- Sew handles on each side with embroidery floss.

- Sew small pockets inside on each narrow end.

- Sew zipper to large pocket. See page 15.

- Sew large pocket to inside of back panel.

- Add any embellishments you like!

Back

Abbreviations

approx	approximately
beg	begin(ning)
bl(s)	back loop(s)
CC	contrasting color
ch(s)	chain(s)
cont	continue, continuing
dc	double crochet
dec	decrease(s), decreasing
EOR	every other row
fl(s)	front loop(s)
inc	increase(s), increasing
MC	main color
m	meters
mm	millimeters
patt	pattern
pm	place marker
rem	remaining
rep(s)	repeat(s)
rnd(s)	round(s)
RS	right side(s)
sc	single crochet
sc2tog	single crochet 2 stitches together
sk	skip
sl st	slip stitch
sp	space
st(s)	stitch(es)
tog	together
WS	wrong side(s)

Useful Information

The size of hooks used in my projects is larger than recommended for these yarns. Due to the nature of the crocheted stitch, the fabric feels bulky after felting. Therefore, I generally used one strand of wool for my bags (and no bulky yarns) unless I wanted a strong, textured look.

If you want to substitute yarns, I would recommend making a test swatch and felting to see how the yarn works. Also note that crochet felts more in width than in height.

CROCHET HOOKS

This is an abbreviated list of the crochet hooks used in this book and their equivalents.

Metric Size Range	U.S. Size Range
5 mm	H-8
5.5 mm	I-9
6 mm	J-10
6.5 mm	K-10½
8 mm	L-11
9 mm	M/N-13
10 mm	N/P-15

STANDARD YARN-WEIGHT SYSTEM

In this book, project yarns are labeled with yarn-weight categories compiled by the Craft Yarn Council of America. Refer to the chart below for descriptions of the various categories.

Yarn-Weight Symbol and Category Names	1 SUPER FINE	2 FINE	3 LIGHT	4 MEDIUM	5 BULKY	6 SUPER BULKY
Types of Yarns in Category	Sock, Fingering, Baby	Sport, Baby	DK, Light Worsted	Worsted, Afghan, Aran	Chunky, Craft, Rug	Bulky, Roving
Crochet Gauge Ranges in Single Crochet to 4"	21 to 32 sts	16 to 20 sts	12 to 17 sts	11 to 14 sts	8 to 11 sts	5 to 9 sts
Recommended Hook in Metric Size Range	2.25 to 3.5 mm	3.5 to 4.5 mm	4.5 to 5.5 mm	5.5 to 6.5 mm	6.5 to 9 mm	9 mm and larger
Recommended Hook in U.S. Size Range	B-1 to E-4	E-4 to 7	7 to I-9	I-9 to K-10½	K-10½ to M-13	M-13 and larger

SKILL LEVEL

You will find the following icons indicating skill level on most patterns. Refer to these to help you choose a pattern that is appropriate for you.

Beginner: Projects for first-time crocheters using basic stitches, minimal shaping.

Easy: Projects using yarn or thread with basic stitches; repetitive stitch patterns; simple color changes, shaping, and finishing.

Intermediate: Projects using a variety of techniques, such as basic lace patterns or color patterns; midlevel shaping and finishing.

Experienced: Projects with intricate stitch patterns, techniques, and dimension, such as nonrepeating patterns, multicolor techniques, detailed shaping, and refined finishing; use of fine threads and small hooks.

Resources

Please contact the following companies to find shops that carry the yarn and accessories featured in this book.

Ann Geddes Studio
www.geddesstudio.com
Glass buttons

Berroco, Inc.
www.berroco.com
Suede

Bryson Distributing
www.brysonknits.com
Clover Needle Felting Tool Kit

Cascade Yarns
www.cascadeyarns.com
Cascade 220

Crystal Palace Yarns
www.straw.com
Fizz, Fizz Stardust

Gay Bowles Sales, Inc.
www.millhillbeads.com
Beads

GGH
www.ggh-garn.de/index_en.php
Strass stones

Gita Maria
www.gitamaria.com
Enamel buttons

Knitting Fever, Inc.
www.knittingfever.com
Aurora, Kureyon, and Silk Garden Lite by Noro; Gatsby by Katia

Leisure Arts, Inc.
www.leisurearts.com
Handles, key rings

Muench Yarns
www.muenchyarns.com
Touch Me, buttons

South West Trading Company
www.soysilk.com
Karaoke, Rhinestone Zipper

Sunbelt Fastener Co.
www.sunbeltfashion.com
Handles, snaps, buckles, grommets

Tahki/Stacy Charles
www.tahkistacycharles.com
127 Print, New Smoking

Westminster Trading for Julia (Nashua Handknits)
www.westminsterfibers.com

Your local craft stores
Buttons, beads, and purse accessories

About the AUTHOR

Eva Wiechmann was born in Finland, a country of long, cold winters and summers with midnight sun. Eva learned to knit and crochet at the age of four. After graduating from school and a 17-year stopover in Germany, she came to America with her husband and daughter in 1984. Since 1987, she has been the owner of Eva's Needlework in Thousand Oaks, California.

At Eva's shop, every knitter and needleworker can feel at home. The excitement is catching when you walk into this store packed with yarn. Eva's Needlework was featured in a knitting publication as one of America's premier shops, which made Eva and her loyal customers very proud.

Eva is the author of *Pursenalities: 20 Great Knitted and Felted Bags* (Martingale & Company, 2004) and *Pursenality Plus: 20 New Felted Bags* (Martingale & Company, 2006).

Knitting and Crochet Titles

Martingale® & COMPANY

America's Best-Loved Craft & Hobby Books®
America's Best-Loved Knitting Books®

CROCHET

Creative Crochet *NEW!*

Crochet for Babies and Toddlers

Crochet for Tots

Crochet from the Heart

Crocheted Socks!

Crocheted Sweaters

Cute Crochet for Kids *NEW!*

The Essential Book of Crochet Techniques

Eye-Catching Crochet

First Crochet

Fun and Funky Crochet

Funky Chunky Crocheted Accessories *NEW!*

The Little Box of Crocheted Bags

The Little Box of Crocheted Hats and Scarves

The Little Box of Crocheted Ponchos and Wraps

More Crocheted Aran Sweaters

KNITTING

200 Knitted Blocks

365 Knitting Stitches a Year: Perpetual Calendar

Big Knitting

Blankets, Hats, and Booties

Dazzling Knits

Double Exposure

Everyday Style

Fair Isle Sweaters Simplified

First Knits

Fun and Funky Knitting

Funky Chunky Knitted Accessories

Handknit Style

Handknit Style II *NEW!*

Knits from the Heart

Knits, Knots, Buttons, and Bows

Knitted Shawls, Stoles, and Scarves

The Knitter's Book of Finishing Techniques

Lavish Lace

The Little Box of Knits for Baby *NEW!*

The Little Box of Knitted Ponchos and Wraps

The Little Box of Knitted Throws

The Little Box of Scarves

The Little Box of Scarves II

The Little Box of Sweaters

Modern Classics *NEW!*

Perfectly Brilliant Knits

The Pleasures of Knitting

Pursenalities

Pursenality Plus

Ribbon Style

Romantic Style

Sarah Dallas Knitting

Saturday Sweaters

Sensational Knitted Socks

Silk Knits *NEW!*

Simply Beautiful Sweaters

The Ultimate Knitted Tee

The Yarn Stash Workbook

Our books are available at bookstores and your favorite craft, fabric, and yarn retailers. If you don't see the title you're looking for, visit us at **www.martingale-pub.com** or contact us at:

1-800-426-3126

International: 1-425-483-3313 • Fax: 1-425-486-7596 • Email: info@martingale-pub.com

10/06 Knit